English Language Teaching Games

for Adult Students

1 Elementary

L. A. Hill
R. D. S. Fielden

Evans Brothers Limited

Published by Evans Brothers Limited
Montague House, Russell Square
London WC1B 5BX

Evans Brothers (Nigeria Publishers) Limited
PMB 5164, Jericho Road
Ibadan

© L. A. Hill and R. D. S. Fielden 1974

All Rights Reserved. No part of this publication may be reproduced, stored in a retrieval system, or transmitted in any form or by any means, electronic, mechanical, photocopying, recording or otherwise, without the prior permission of Evans Brothers Limited.

First published 1974
Fifth impression 1979

Set, printed and bound in Great Britain by
Fakenham Press Limited, Fakenham, Norfolk
ISBN 0 237 49880 4

PRA 6783

Introduction

The purpose of this book is to provide teachers of English as a foreign or second language with games which they can use in class to help adult students to improve their command of the more important and common structures (sentence patterns) of English. The games dealing with the more elementary structures are in Book 1, and those dealing with the more advanced ones in Book 2. The selection of the structures to be included in each book was based on previous work done by L. A. Hill.

In each game, the teacher is first given the structures it is intended to give practice in. As it is important not only to have a good command of an individual structure, but also to know when to use that one and when to use another with which it might be confused, the point which is practised in each game is a *contrast* between two or more structures. For example, in Game 18 on pages 33 and 34, the students are given practice in choosing between the present continuous and the present simple tenses. The work is therefore *contrastive*, and it is also *contextualized*, since each choice between contrasting structures arises from the context in which it is used.

Since this is a teacher's and not a student's book, the teacher is given suggestions for carrying on each game, and a few examples, but he is not given every single sentence he can use during it. This leaves him (or her; the reference to a teacher of one sex will always imply equally the other) plenty of scope for using his own imagination, and for bringing in vocabulary which the student knows and which is of local interest.

Games in the classroom

Now a word about games in the classroom. In recent years our understanding of the place of motivation, anxiety and enjoyment in learning has grown. Adults usually have enough motivation to learn a new language. Though they are often unrealistic about the time and effort needed to make progress, they seldom need additional pressure from the teacher. What most often interferes with their progress is anxiety about their ability to learn a new skill. This perhaps arises from previous difficulty with the subject; or because of the misleading saying, which is found in some form in most cultures, 'You can't teach an old dog new tricks'; or – the commonest reason of all – because memories of school are not pleasant. A return to the classroom brings back these memories. This is particularly likely if the way the room is arranged and the way the teacher behaves remind the student sharply of what he feels to be the most typical of that situation. The picture on the next page will most easily make this clear.

Because of this, there is now an emphasis on the teacher, and the institution in

which he teaches, working to create a more informal atmosphere, and on enjoyment as a positive factor in overcoming anxiety. Little learning of a new language can take place without practice. In the classroom the shy student tends to get less practice and to become more embarrassed as time goes on. The teacher may be aware of this, but he also knows that if he draws attention to it – by direct questioning, for example – he may cause further embarrassment. If the teacher can create situations like those suggested in this book, such students will find themselves drawn into an atmosphere in which they can forget about their lack of confidence and begin to take part alongside the less shy or the more competent students.

In this book it is often suggested that the class should be divided into smaller groups. If the classes you have are large – 25 students, or more – it will be found of benefit to divide the class even where this is not mentioned. It gives more practice to more people and helps to overcome the ordeal, for some, of speaking in front of so many others. When the class is divided, the teacher's role changes. While in the situation illustrated above he can only teach the group as one, with all the students working on the same task, in group activity he can set tasks which may differ according to need. He may have a group for people who are having one particular problem, or of students who were absent when an important structure was dealt with. The teacher's job is now to go round the groups, listen carefully and only interfere if a group appears to have misunderstood the task itself, or is making a serious mistake which no member of the group appears to have noticed.

However, it is usually found that in a group of from five to eight people, some member will recognize and draw attention to such a mistake. The teacher can help, or hinder, this by his behaviour. If he is looked upon as the only person who knows what is right and wrong, then members will tend to avoid helping others to recognize the same. If, on the other hand, he shows that he expects the group's members to help each other, this responsibility is more widely shared, and each group can become responsible for its own standard.

Though this book is written with the needs of adult learners in mind, much of the material will be found appropriate for younger students.

With such groups, the competitive element of games could be emphasized. On the whole, there is evidence that adult learners are not very interested in competing with others; they are much more concerned with coming up to their own standard, so you will have to be cautious in pressing this aspect with them. With children, however, it could add interest and excitement to the classroom. In any case, we would like to emphasize again the need to adapt to the circumstances of the teacher's own country, style of teaching and situation.

Some games may take only a few minutes to play. Those which have several steps will take longer. You are recommended to use the complete game, as the later steps build on the earlier, though each step is complete in itself. Suggestions are made from time to time for developing the game.

To sum up, games are an admirable way to practise language. Because they place speech in a social context, the student is encouraged to use all his linguistic knowledge *actively*. Occasionally the games may appear to introduce an artificial element into the situation, but almost all are taken from situations found outside the classroom. This ability to bring life into the classroom makes them so valuable to language teachers and learners.

L.A.H. & R.D.S.F.

Game 1

Structures

A[n])(*the*

Structural Notes

The is used before nouns which refer to people/animals/things which are the only ones in the particular situation being dealt with; e.g. we say *the sun* in most cases, because it is the only one in our universe; *the floor* because it is the only one in the room we are talking about; *the first boy in this row* because there is only one first boy in the row.

A[n] is used before singular countable nouns when we mean 'one of that class of noun which we call a[n] . . .'; e.g. *a boy, a horse, an apple.*

Materials

1. Stories and picture stories containing plenty of objects which can be referred to using *the* or *a*; e.g. *That's the sea* or *That's a ship.*
2. Instruction sheet, see Step 2 below.

Method

Step 1 (a)   The teacher points to various objects, some of which are unique, others not. Students have to say what they are, using *a* or *the*; e.g.

Teacher   (pointing to the sun in picture): What's that?
Student A   It's the sun.
Teacher   And what's that?
Student B   It's a star.

The teacher can use, for example, *the sun, the moon, the sky, the sea, the land, the seaside, the equator.*

Step 1 (b)   Here we go on to things which are unique only in a particular situation; e.g. in a classroom we have only one

Teacher	ceiling and floor; often we also have only one blackboard and only one teacher's table. We then usually refer to these as *the ceiling, the floor*, etc. (pointing to the only window in his classroom, or in a picture of a classroom): Here's a classroom. What's this?
Student A	It's the window.
Teacher	(pointing to one of the doors in the classroom): And what's this?
Student B	It's a door.
	By using more than one picture (e.g. of various classrooms), the teacher can get the students sometimes to say *the blackboard* and sometimes to say *a blackboard*, for example (the first when there is only one in the place, the other when there is more than one).
Step 1 (c)	Instead of showing pictures, the teacher can set the situation by what he says; e.g.
Teacher	I am thinking about a garden. There is a tree in the middle of it, and there are four bushes, one in each corner. There is only one tree in the garden, but there are four bushes. Now John's hiding in the middle of the garden. Where's he hiding, A?
Student A	Behind the tree.
Teacher	Now he's hiding in one of the corners of the garden. Where's he hiding, B?
Student B	Behind a bush.
Step 1 (d)	Here we go on to *the* before things already mentioned; e.g. *There's a boy and a girl here. The boy's name is Peter, and the girl's is Joan.* The teacher can show pictures of different people, animals and things and then get the students to ask questions about them; e.g. the teacher shows a picture of a horse and another of a cow.
Teacher	A, ask B what this is.
Student A	What's that, B?
Student B	It's a horse.
Teacher	Now ask D what this is, C.
Student C	What's this, D?
Student D	It's a cow.
Teacher	E, ask F a question about colour.
Student E	What colour's the horse, F?
Student F	The horse is brown.
Teacher	Another question about colour, G.
Student G	What colour's the cow, H?
Student H	The cow's black and white.
	The teacher can also use the blackboard; e.g.
Teacher	(drawing a box): What's this?
Student A	It's a box.

Teacher	(drawing a bucket): And what's this?
Student B	It's a bucket.
Teacher	(drawing a star on the box): What have I done now?
Student C	You've drawn a star on the box.
Teacher	(drawing the lid of the box open): And what have I done now?
Student D	You've opened the box.
Step 1 (e)	Here we do *the* in *on the left, on the right, in the middle* and in superlatives; e.g.
Teacher	(drawing three chairs on the blackboard): This chair is big. And what is this one?
Student A	It's bigger.
Teacher	Yes. And this one?
Student B	It's the biggest.
Teacher	Which chair is the smallest?
Student C	The one in the middle.
Teacher	And which is the biggest?
Student D	The one on the right.
Teacher	And the one on the left?
Student E	The one on the left is bigger than the one in the middle, but it's smaller than the one on the right.
Step 2	For the game, divide the class into teams of four, with two teams to each table and a scorer for each team. The picture shows how you might arrange the classroom.

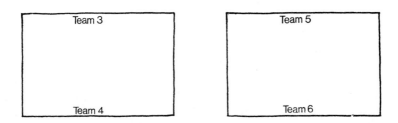

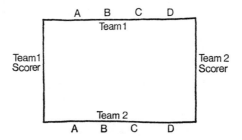

The scorer acts as chairman of his team and takes charge of the materials for the game.

For example, in the first round you want the teams to practise the structures in the way you have already done in Step 1 (a) above. You will have to provide a picture for each table and a sheet of instructions for each scorer. (These can be the same for every table.) The first might read:

Round 1	Point to objects in the picture and ask members of the opposing team in turn to say what they are, using *a* or *the*. This round lasts until each member of both teams has answered one question correctly; e.g.
Team 1 Scorer	What's that?
Team 2 Student A	It's a road.
Scorer	Right. You get 1 point.

If the scorer, or any member of his team, thinks the wrong answer has been given, he says so. In that case Team 1 would get the point. However, if the other team challenges this, they must ask the teacher. He should move round the room to see that the games are running smoothly.

The next question is asked by Team 2 Scorer, and so on until the end of the round, when both scores are added up.

It is not necessary to have a round for each section of Step 1. The game could be played on several occasions; in this case the same instructions can be used with a different picture each time.

Game 2

Structures

A/an)(no article

Structural Notes

For *a/an*, see Game 1.
When a noun is uncountable, we do not put *a[n]* before it; e.g. we say *I want water, not bread*. We do not say *a water* or *a bread*, because we do not count water and bread: we measure or weigh it.

Materials

1. Several sets of cards. On each card you should put a noun which gives your students trouble with *a/an*.
2. A separate list of all the nouns in each set of cards, in random order, without *a/an*.
3. A similar list of all the nouns in each set of cards, but arranged in such a way that all those with *a/an* are in one column and all those without in another.

Examples of cards: | POEM | POETRY | CLIMATE | WEATHER |

Example of part of the list without *a/an*: chalk
dentist
headache
jewel
jewellery
music

Example of part of the same list, divided up into nouns which take *a/an* and those which do not:

a/an	–
dentist	chalk
headache	jewellery
jewel	music

5

Method

Divide the class up into teams of between five and eight students. Two teams play against each other in each case.

Give the leader of each team (i) one of the sets of cards (see Materials 1 above); (ii) a list of the words in his opponents' set of cards, without *a/an* (see Materials 2 above); (iii) a list of the words in his own set, divided into those with *a/an* and those with nothing (see Materials 3 above).

The leader of each team should then deal his set of cards out to the members of his team and put the list of his opponents' words where all his own team can see it and the list of his own team's words face down on the table.

The teams now take turns to ask for a card from their opponents' set. To win a card, they have to make a correct sentence using the word they want; e.g.

First Member of Team 1 (seeing the word *bicycle* on the list of his opponents' words): Who can give me a bicycle?
The Member of Team 2 who has BICYCLE: I can. (He gives the card to his opponent, who puts it on the table in front of him.) Now who can give me furniture?
The Member of Team 1 who has FURNITURE: I can. (He gives it). Who can play music?
The Member of Team 2 who has MUSIC: I can. (He gives it). Who wants to be a dentist?
The Member of Team 1 who has DENTIST: I do. (He gives the card.)

The teacher has to decide, before the game begins, whether only mistakes in the structure being practised should be challenged or all kinds of mistakes.

If a student asks a question incorrectly, the opposing team can challenge him. Then, by looking at his list (which is marked with *a/an*), the leader of the challenged team can see who is right. If the challenger is correct, the student who made the mistake has to give one of his cards to him and lose his turn. The card which he gives is put on the table in front of the successful challenger. If the challenger is wrong, he has to give up the card for which the student who was correct asked and also lose his turn.

The team which has the greatest number of cards in front of it at the end of the time allowed by the teacher is the winner.

Game 3

Structures

Phrases with the definite article; e.g. *go to the office*)(phrases without it; e.g. *go to school*

Structural Notes

There are idiomatic prepositional phrases in English in which *the* is used; e.g. *I am going to the office, I have a pain in the leg, I go to the barber's once a month, We sleep during the night*; and others in which *the* is not used; e.g. *I am going to school, I came by bus, We sleep at night*.

Materials

1. Sentences containing the structures, but with *the* omitted where it normally occurs; e.g.
   John is at . . . home.
   Ali is at . . . mosque.
   I came here by . . . bus.
   I came here in . . . school bus.
2. Questions, statements and pictures which can stimulate students to use the structures (see Steps 1 (b) and 2 below).
3. Instruction sheets and blank cards (see Step 2 below).

Method

Step 1 (a)   Give the students sentences like those in Materials 1 above and get them to write out the complete sentences, putting *the* instead of the blanks where necessary.

Step 1 (b)   Make statements, ask questions, point to pictures or do actions to encourage students to respond using one of the structures; e.g.

Teacher	What are you going to play at two o'clock this afternoon?
Student A	We are going to play football.
Teacher	(pointing to a picture): What is this man playing?
Student B	He is playing the piano.
Teacher	(holding his stomach): Where have I got a pain?
Student C	You've got a pain in the stomach.

If necessary, you can prompt a student by giving him a noun; e.g.

Teacher	Bill is a thief. Prison.
Student D	Bill is a thief. He will go to prison.

Step 2   In this game students work in teams of two or three and carry out instructions you have prepared. Arrange the room as in the illustration.

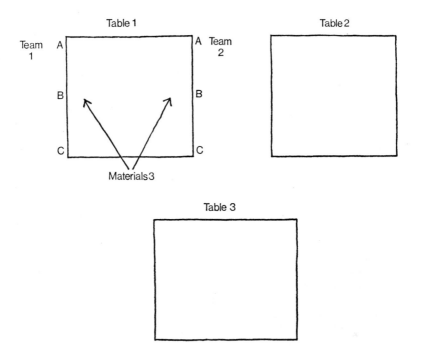

Tell the teams to write questions about a picture, or to work out questions to ask after pointing at the picture or at something or someone in the room or after doing actions. Give the teams time to do this before telling them to start play.

    Student A in Team 1 then puts the first question to his opponent. If the answer given is accepted, Team 2 gains one point, but if it is not accepted, Team 1 must give its own answer and gains two points if Team 2 accepts this. A team which challenges a correct answer loses one point. The teacher is called in to decide if the teams disagree.

Game 4

Structures

Plurals with *-s*)(unchanged plurals)(plurals with *pieces of*; e.g.
These are | tables
fish
pieces of furniture

Structural Notes

Most nouns in English form their plural by adding *-s*; e.g. *dog, dogs*; *plate, plates*. Some which end in a hissing sound add *-es*; e.g. *church, churches*; *class, classes* Some nouns have irregular plurals; e.g. *knife, knives*; *man, men*; *child, children* Some nouns do not change in the plural; e.g. *sheep, sheep*; *fish, fish*; *deer, deer*.
Some uncountable nouns (see Game 2 above) have a kind of plural with *pieces of*; e.g. we can say *There is some furniture in this room*, but not *There are some furnitures*. However, we can say, *There are some pieces of furniture*.

Materials

Several dice; pictures and sentences, either duplicated or on the blackboard (see examples in Method below).

Method

For this game, arrange the class in a circle, with a table in the centre. You need enough dice to make the total number of students in your class; e.g. if you have 18 students, you need three dice (3×6). Before starting the game, give each student a number; e.g. Student A is 1, Student B is 2. The teacher throws one or more of the dice at the start and calls out the total; e.g. if he throws he calls 'Number Ten'. The student with that number then has to run to the central table and answer the next question on the duplicated sheet or on the blackboard.

Examples:

1.

This man is tall, but ...   (woman)*

2.

The watches in this window are cheap, but the ...   (jewellery)*
3. I don't like beer, but most ...   (people)*
4. English is easy, but mathematics ...
5.

This crab is small, but ...

*These words must be used in the answers, either in the singular or in the plural.
   When the student has answered correctly, he throws the dice and calls the number of the next person. But if he fails to answer correctly, he has to answer the question which has the number of the dice he throws; e.g. if he throws a total of 15, he has to answer question 15.

Game 5

Structures

Who is . . . ?)(*What is . . . ?*)(*Who are . . . ?*)(*What are . . . ?*

Structural Notes

Who refers to persons, *what* to animals and things. An exception is the type of question '*What is that man?*' '*He is a barber*' compared with '*Who is that man?*' '*It is Mr Jones*'.
   It is singular, *are* is plural; e.g. *Who is that man? Who are those men?*

Materials

A large box containing small unbreakable objects collected from students (or others). The teacher should decide on appropriate objects in the light of the vocabulary level of his class. Some objects could be used for teaching new vocabulary later in the lesson. Ensure that some objects are plural (e.g. keys, pencils held together by a rubber band) so that all structures may be practised.

Method

Step 1 (a)	Student A is blindfolded. A second student, B, is *silently* called out. Student A must try to guess who it is, the class saying whether he is right or wrong; e.g.
Student B	Who is this?
Student A	It's C.
Class	No, it isn't.
Teacher	Ask another question, B.
Student B	Who am I?
Student A	It's B.
Class	Right.
Teacher	Now move on to the second part.
Step 1 (b)	Student B takes an object from the box and drops it on the desk.

Student B	What's this?
Student A	It's a piece of chalk.
Class	No, it isn't.
Student A	It's a pen.
Class	Yes, it is.

At this point A and B return to their seats and another pair play the same game. Make sure that the first student is blindfolded before the second is called out.

Step 2   After a few minutes, it is possible to divide the class into groups, each performing the second part (b) of Step 1 above.

In this case smaller collections of objects would be necessary, but they must be hidden in a box or under a cloth. The teacher should observe how the groups are managing and go to the help of any which appear to be in difficulty.

Game 6

Structures

Personal pronouns as subjects)(personal pronouns as objects

Structural Notes

I/me refers to the speaker/writer; *we/us* to the speaker/writer plus one or more other people; *you* to the person[s] spoken/written to; *he/him/she/her/they/them* to any other person[s].

He/him refers to one male person; *she/her* to one female person; and *they/them* to two or more people.

I/we/you/he/she/they is the subject of the verb; *me/us/you/him/her/them* is the object of the verb or preposition. The complement of the verb *to be*, e.g. *I/me* in *It is I* and *It's me*, is *I/we/he/she/they* in formal English but *me/us/him/her/them* in everyday English.

Materials

Names of some of your students, followed by sentences about those students and others; e.g.

John

John	hit Peter.	Fred pushed	John.
	shook hands with George.	Mary listened to	
	talked to Helen.	Joan helped	

If you know your students well, you can make these quite funny.

Method

Step 1 (a)   Get John to answer some questions about the statements on the blackboard; e.g.
Teacher   What did you do to Peter?
John   I hit him.
Teacher   And what did you do to George?
John   I shook hands with him.
Teacher   What did Fred do to you?
John   He pushed me.

Step 1 (b)   Ask Peter, George, Helen, etc., questions; e.g.
Teacher   What did John do to you, George?
George   He shook hands with me.
Teacher   What did you do to John, Mary?
Mary   I listened to him.

Step 1 (c)   Ask other students questions about the sentences on the blackboard; e.g.
Teacher   What did John do to Helen?
Student A He talked to her.
Teacher   What did Joan do to John?
Student B She helped him.

You can also practise *we*, *us* and *them* by putting two names on the blackboard instead of one; e.g. (on the blackboard) *John and Peter pushed Mary and Helen.*

Teacher   What did John and Peter do to you and Helen, Mary?
Mary   They pushed us.

Step 2   Further practice could be given by making instruction sheets for two teams to a table and playing and scoring as in Game 1, Step 2.

Game 7

Structures

Possessive pronouns and nouns in the possessive; e.g.
  Whose is this? It's *mine*
  Whose are these/those? They're *John's/those boys'*

Structural Notes

A singular noun takes *'s* to make it possessive; e.g. *the boy's book, This is the boy's.* A plural noun takes *'*; e.g. *the boys' books, Those are the boys'.*
  I, we, you, he, she, it, they, who become *my, our, your, his, her, its, their, whose,* respectively, when they come before a noun; e.g. *my book, its tail, whose house;* and *mine, ours, yours, his, hers, —*, theirs, whose* when not followed by a noun; e.g. *This is ours. Whose is that?*
*Its must always be followed by a noun: we cannot say **This is its.*

Materials and Method

The room should be arranged, if possible, so that there is a table in the middle.

Each student should bring a small object and put it on the table (see note in Game 5 about the problem of vocabulary). If your class is larger than 15, take away objects until there are 15 on the table. Cover them with a cloth.

Step 1	Uncover the objects.
Teacher	(picking up a ruler): Whose is this?
Student A	It's mine.
Teacher	It's Alan's. What is it? (Anyone except A is allowed to answer.)
Student B	It's Alan's ruler.

Other students can come out to act as the teacher. The teacher prompts and corrects. This step prepares the structures and revises the vocabulary for Step 2.

Step 2   *Kim's Game.* Re-arrange the objects on the table, adding some and taking others away to leave not more than 15. Ask the students to gather round the table: it is most important that all should be able to see equally well.

Uncover the objects for one minute, then cover again. Ask everyone to return to their seats and write down as many objects as they can remember. Allow no longer than four minutes. Ask them to draw a line under the last item and add up the number of objects listed.

Step 3	Returning the objects.
Teacher	(or it could be done by a student): Whose is this?
Student C	It's mine. *Or* That's my ruler.
Teacher	Who hasn't put *ruler* on his list? ... Please write it under the line on your paper. The others tick that item above their line.

In this way all the items are checked. Note that it is possible for a student to have remembered an item from Step 1 which may not have appeared on the table for Step 2; this would lose one point. The student with the highest number of points wins.

Game 8

Structures

He/him/his)(*she/her/hers*

Structural Notes

See Game 6, paragraph 2.

Materials

Pictures for work in groups; see Step 1.

Method

Step 1 — Students have to talk about fellow students and/or photographs and pictures. They have first to identify the person and then to make remarks about him/her, using the pronouns given in Structures above; e.g.

Student A — That's George. He's a student. I like him. That's his desk. That chair is his too.

Student B — That's my mother (pointing to a photo). She's 40 years old. My sister and I live with her. Her name's Elizabeth. This bag is hers.

Step 2 — This game will give practice in composition and will also help students to recognize some difficulties with these pronouns by inviting them to make deliberate mistakes for another group to correct. The groups should be small – from three to five students – and should be given a picture like that below. They are asked to write a story based on the picture and to make some of the pronouns wrong, keeping a separate note of the mistakes they have put in.

They then exchange stories with another group and at the same time give the note of the mistakes to the teacher. He should check both these and the stories (he can do this by going round whilst groups are making corrections), but should not interfere at this stage. The group which recognizes all the mistakes wins; if it finds some others as well, these are worth 2 points each.

The teacher should revise with the whole class any mistakes which have been made by more than one group.

Game 9

Structures

Pronouns with *-self/-selves*)(pronouns without *-self/-selves*

Structural Notes

When the object of a verb or preposition is a pronoun and is the same person/animal/thing as the subject of the clause, it usually takes the *-self/-selves* form. *I, you* (singular), *he, she, it, we, you* (plural), *they* and impersonal *one* become *myself, yourself, himself, herself, itself, ourselves, yourselves, themselves* and *oneself*; e.g. *I can see myself in that glass. The boys go to school by themselves.*

The *-self/selves* pronouns can also be added to nouns and pronouns for emphasis; e.g. *You yourself often go out alone* or *You often go out alone yourself.*

Materials

Captioned pictures about which statements can be made (see Method Step 1 below).

Method

Step 1   The teacher points to a picture and gets one of the students to make a statement about it, using any word which is in brackets after it; e.g.

1. This is Bill. (washing)   2. This is Bill and his mother. (washing)

The teacher points to Picture 1.
Student A   This is Bill. He is washing himself.
The teacher points to Picture 2.
Student B   This is Bill and his mother. She is washing him.
Students then have to pretend they are the people in the pictures and to make the statements accordingly; e.g.
Teacher   C, you are Bill, and D, you are Bill's mother. (He points to Picture 1.)
Student C   I'm washing myself.
The teacher points to Picture 2.
Student C   My mother's washing me.
Student D then says to C: I'm washing you.

Step 2 (a)   Ask each student to pretend to be a journalist and to make up a report about something he saw happening. In each report, each of the *-self/selves* pronouns should appear at least once.

Step 2 (b)   Divide the students into pairs to give practice to everyone at the same time. Student A reads his report to Student B as if he was doing it over the telephone, while B takes down some notes. Then B reads his report to A.

Step 2 (c)   Each student writes a report for a newspaper in the third person; brief quotations in the first person are allowed.

Get all the students to read their reports out to the class if possible. The class can vote on which report they consider the clearest and most interesting. If there isn't time to read all the reports, divide the class into groups and get all the students in each group to read their reports to the others in the group. Each group can choose the reports it thinks the best, and those can then be read out to the whole class.

Game 10

Structures

Some)(*any*)(*none*; e.g.

I've got *some* | water
books

Have you got *any* | water?
books?

I haven't got *any* | water?
books

I've got | *some*
none

Have you got *any*?
I haven't got *any*

Structural Notes

Some is used before or instead of plural and uncountable nouns in affirmative sentences; e.g. *I want some bananas/money. John wants some too. Any* replaces *some* in negative and interrogative sentences; e.g. *I don't want any bananas/money. John doesn't want any either. Do you want any [bananas/money]?*

None means 'not any'; e.g. *I have none* means 'I haven't any'. It is not used before a noun.

Materials
Objects for Step 1 below.
Three blank cards for each student for Step 2.

Method

Step 1 — Give each student a different collection of objects or pictures of objects; e.g. a few stones, books and pencils, a bottle of ink, a bottle of water, a small tin of sand. Then write the name of an object, e.g. *book* or *milk*, on the blackboard.

One student then has to ask the others whether they have any, and they have to answer.

Student A   Have you got any books?
Student B   Yes, I've got some books *or* Yes, I've got some.
Student C   No, I haven't got any books *or* I have no books *or* I haven't got any *or* I've got none.

You can make it a rule that the different kinds of answers, e.g. *I've got some water* and *I've got some,* have to be used alternately; e.g. if one student says *I haven't got any books,* the next one who hasn't got any has to say *I have no books,* the next has to say *I haven't got any,* etc.

Step 2   This game can be played with the whole class if it isn't too large, and with a good atmosphere it can create quite a lot of humour.

Make up and write out beforehand a story, freely using these structures. Arrange the class in a circle, give all students three blank cards and ask them to write *SOME* on one, *ANY* on the next and *NONE* on the third.

Now tell the story, but when you reach any of these words say *blank* instead of it. When it is clear which is the correct word, call out a name. The student called must without delay hold up the right card. As there are three cards for two hands, this should give quite a lot of fun. E.g.

Teacher   Here is the story with *blank* in place of these words. Show the correct card to fill in the blank. 'I went to the shop this morning to buy *blank* apples.' Student A.

Without delay Student A should hold up his *SOME* card. If he cannot make up his mind the teacher should call 'What do you think, Student B?'.

Teacher   'I was unlucky because when I got there they hadn't *blank*. They had sold out.' Student C.

Student C should hold up his *ANY* card.

Game 11

Structures

A lot [of])(*much*)(*many*)(*a little*)(*a few*; e g.

(I've got) *a lot* [*of* | water / books]

(I haven't got) | *much* / *many* [water / books]

(Have you got) | *much* / *many* [water / books] ? / ?

(I've got) | *a little* [water] / *a few* [books]

Structural Notes

A lot of is used before plural and uncountable nouns in affirmative sentences; e.g. *I have a lot of bananas/money*. *A lot* (without *of*) is used in such sentences when no noun follows; e.g. *John has a lot too*.

Many replaces *a lot of* before plural nouns, and *a lot* when no noun follows but a plural noun is understood in negative and interrogative sentences; e.g. *I haven't got many bananas. Have you got many?*

Much replaces *a lot of* before uncountable nouns, and *a lot* when no noun follows but an uncountable noun is understood; e.g. *I haven't got much money. Have you got much?*

Materials

1. Anything which can easily be changed in quantity; e.g. two jugs, one filled and one empty; a pile of paper or of small books; a bundle of pencils or small sticks. These should be given out to various students.
2. Instruction cards for Step 2.

Method
Step 1
Teacher (keeping two or three books from the pile) Have I got many books, Student A?
Student A No, you haven't.
Teacher Has Student B got many [books]? (B has the rest of the pile)
Student A Yes, he has a lot [of books].

Step 2
When the teacher has practised all the structures with the class, he should organize groups of five around different collections with instruction cards, listing different ways of using the collection; e.g.
the collection is a bundle of pencils and the two jugs, one full and the other empty. One person, A, is to be the leader who reads the instructions to the others. Give three pencils to B and nine to C.
Student A (to D) Has B or C got many pencils?
Student D B has a few pencils, C has a lot.
Now divide C's bundle equally between C and D and continue. You will be able to think of ways of bringing in all the structures and of giving practice to all the members in each group. The same instruction card will do for each group if you are able to organize the same collection for each; or if the different collections contain similar kinds of objects, e.g. instead of the bundle of pencils in the example use a bundle of sticks.

Game 12

Structures

A little)(*a few*

Structural Notes

A few is used before or instead of plural nouns; e.g. *I have a few bananas. John has a few too.*
   A little is used before or instead of uncountable nouns, e.g. *I have a little money. John has a little too.*

Materials

Sentences using *a little* and *a few* but with these words omitted and also questions to be answered with them. It will help if the separate sentences and questions are put on cards and handed out.

Method

Step 1   The teacher asks a student to read out his sentence and give the missing word; e.g.

Teacher   Could we have your sentence, A?
Student A   I have only . . . money left. (a little)

Alternatively:
Teacher   Could you ask B your question, A?
Student A   Are there any beans left?
Student B   A few.

Step 2
Continue this in pairs or threes.

Game 13

Structures

Big, bigger)(*bigger than*)(*the biggest*)(*a big —*)(*a bigger —*

Structural Notes

Short adjectives and adverbs tend to form their comparative by adding *-er*, and their superlative by adding *-est*, e.g. *cold, colder, the coldest* and *quickly, quicker, the quickest*; sometimes with some spelling modifications, e.g. *fat, fatter, the fattest*; *pretty, prettier, the prettiest*; *wide, wider, the widest*.

Longer adjectives and adverbs tend to form their comparatives with *more*, and their superlatives with *most*; e.g. *interesting, more interesting, the most interesting*; *easily, more easily, the most easily*.

Materials

A coloured picture of a garden, the countryside or a town which is large enough for the whole class to see, and also a number of smaller ones for groups.

Method

Step 1	The teacher starts by asking questions about size, quality or colour.
Teacher	Is this a big tree/garden/house?
Student A	Yes, it is *or* No, it isn't *or* No, but it is bigger than the other tree.
Teacher	Right. Come out to ask the next question.
Student A	Student B, which is the biggest car?

In the whole group the teacher will be able to check the use of these structures and should ensure that the full range is practised.

Step 2   This question and answer work should now be continued in groups of between five and seven, using smaller pictures and different situations. Make sure that the picture contains plenty of contrasts of colour, size, shape and quality.

If a competitive atmosphere between groups is desired, it is possible to make the winner the group which continues longest, without repeating any comparisons.

Game 14

Structures

Adjectives)(adverbs

Structural Notes

One can change most adjectives into adverbs by adding *-ly*; e.g. *nice, nicely; careful, carefully*.
  Sometimes there is a change of spelling too; e.g. *happy, happily; dull, dully*. *Good* becomes *well*.
  Sometimes the adverb is the same as the adjective; e.g. *fast; low*.

Materials
Lists of questions (see Method Step 1 below); lists of adjectives (see Method Step 2).

Method

Step 1 — Ask questions, some of which require adjectives and others adverbs in their answers. Choose questions which test difficulties which you know your students have in choosing between adjectives and adverbs; e.g.

Teacher How do you feel when you have passed an examination?
Student A I feel happy.
Teacher And how do you tell your parents about your success?
Student B I tell them happily.
Teacher How does ice feel?
Student C It feels cold.
Teacher How do you feel someone's arm when it may be broken?
Student D I feel it carefully.

Step 2 — The teacher asks someone to mime an action in a certain way, using one of the adjectives on the blackboard as the basis of his adverb; e.g.

Teacher What is A doing?
Student B He is sweeping the floor.
Teacher How is he sweeping the floor?
Student C He is sweeping it quickly.

Then Student C has to perform an action, Student D has to ask the questions instead of the teacher, and Student E has to answer them.

Once an adverb has been used it may not be used again in a later mime.

Game 15

Structures

A long way/time and *far/long*

Structural Notes

See Games 10 and 11, above.
    In affirmative sentences we use *a long way* and *a long time*; e.g. *We went a long way yesterday. We were away a long time.*
    In negative sentences and questions these become *far* and *long* respectively; e.g. *We didn't go far. Did you go far? We weren't away long. Were you away long?*

Materials

Find out the distances from the place where you have your class to various other places; e.g. the post office, the railway station, some villages and towns in your country. Find out approximately how long it takes to get to these places by bus/train/etc., or on foot. Write the names of the places and the times on the blackboard.

Method

Step 1	Practise the structures given above with your class.
Step 2	One student pretends to be a stranger and asks questions. Other students have to answer these. If a student answers correctly, he gets a point; if he answers incorrectly, he changes with the 'stranger'; e.g.
'Stranger'	Excuse me please, is it far to . . . (e.g. the bus stop)?
Student A	Yes, it's a long way.
Student B	No, it isn't far.
'Stranger'	How far is it?
Students A and B	It's about half a kilometre (or whatever the distance written on the board is).

'Stranger'	Does it take long to get there?
Student A	Yes, it takes a long time.
Student B	No, it doesn't take long.
'Stranger'	How long does it take?
Students A and B	It takes a quarter of an hour (or whatever the time written on the board is).

Then another three students do the same with another place, and so on. After the game is finished, the class can be asked to vote on which student gave the best performance and put the greatest amount of expression into what he said.

Game 16

Structures

Am)(*are*)(*is*; e.g.
  Who *am* I? You *are* (Mr. Jones)
  Who *are* you? I'*m* (Mr. Jones)/We'*re* (your students)
  Who'*s* (that man)? He'*s* (Mr. Jones)
                       She'*s* (Miss Jones)
                       It'*s* (Mr. Jones)
                             (Miss Jones)
  Who'*re* (those men)? They'*re* (our friends)

Structural Notes

Am goes with *I*, e.g. *Who am I?*; *are* goes with *we/you/they* or a plural noun/pronoun, e.g. *Who are we/you/they/those/those men?*; *is* goes with *he/she/it* or a singular noun/pronoun, e.g. *Who is he/she/it/that/that man?*

Materials
None

Method

Step 1	The teacher demonstrates a simple mime, e.g. closing the door, and asks the students to say what he is doing; e.g.
Teacher	What am I doing?
Student A	You're closing the door.
Teacher	Right. Now, A, come out and do something. (A comes out and mimes.) What is A doing?
Student B	He's putting a stamp on a letter.
Teacher	Now, B, come out and do something. (B comes out and mimes.) C, what's B doing?
Student C	He's reading a book.

Step 2 — Students take turns to come out and mime. If the teacher points to the student who is miming, that student has to say what he is doing; e.g. *I'm drawing a circle on the blackboard*. If the teacher points to the student who is miming and also to another student, the latter has to tell the first student what he is doing; e.g. 'You're singing'. If the teacher points to himself and one of the students who are not doing the action, this student has to tell the teacher what the first student is doing; e.g. *John's taking his coat off*.

Any student who makes a mistake loses a point for his team. You can also practise *we are* and *they are* by bringing two or more students out at the same time.

Game 17

Structures

Present simple tense: 3rd person singular with -s)(other persons without -s

Structural Notes

The third person singular of the present simple tense takes -s; e.g. *he gives, she wants, it gets.* The other persons of this tense do not take -s; e.g. *I give, you want, we get, they like.*

Instead of -s, we often have -es after hissing sounds; e.g. *miss, misses; push, pushes.*

Sometimes there are spelling changes; e.g. *marry, marries.*

Have becomes *has*; and *can, may, must, ought, shall* and *will* remain unchanged.

Materials

Lists of sentences (see Method Step 1 below); pictures to stimulate a story (see Method Step 2).

Method

Step 1 — Give students sentences to complete, some of which require the third person singular, and others other persons; e.g.

I don't like coffee, but John* ...   (*likes it very much*)
Mary doesn't speak English, but we ...   (*speak it very well*)
Englishmen come from England, but a Scotsman ... (*comes from Scotland*)
Why is Jean* here? Because she ...   (*wants to learn English*)
Why are you here? Because we ...   (*want to learn English*)

Instead of the names marked with *, you can use names of students in your class. Students should be asked to use full verbs (not short answers) in completing the sentences. The words in brackets above are what the students are expected to say and should not be given to the students before the questions are asked.

Step 2   The teacher should explain that this is a shared story about the pictures he has provided. It is to be told in the present tense, as if it is the description of something that occurs habitually, or the description of some process, such as cooking something. One student starts by giving a sentence about the pictures, then another continues with another sentence, and so on.

Divide the class into teams, one to tell the story, the other to look for mistakes. At any point, the second team can challenge what the first group has said; e.g.

Student A   Mistake!
Teacher   What was the mistake?
Student A   X said 'He lift the knife'. The correct sentence is 'He lifts the knife'.

If the challenger is correct, his group gets a point. If he is wrong, it loses a point.

Here is an example of a picture story and some of the sentences which can be made up about it:

This is how we make bread in our village. We take flour and water. We mix them together well. We put in some salt. Then we make loaves. We put the loaves in the oven.

Instead of *we*, you can have *I, you, the women, my mother, our baker*, etc.

Game 18

Structures

Present simple tense)(present continuous tense

Structural Notes

The present simple tense is used mostly for habitual action over a period of time which includes the present, e.g. *I get up at seven every day*.

The present continuous tense is mostly used for actions going on at the time of speaking/writing; e.g. *I am talking to you now. You are listening to me*, but not with 'involuntary' verbs (see Game 20).

Materials

Lists of sentences to be added to (see Method Step 1 below).

Method

Step 1   Make statements using one of the above tenses, to which students have to add statements using the other; e.g.

Teacher   I am wearing black shoes.
Student A   You always wear black shoes.
Teacher   Anna* usually wears a blue dress.
Student B   She is wearing one today; *or* But she is wearing a yellow one today.

The teacher can test the correct use of tenses in the verbs *hate, hope, know, like, love, mean, prefer, remember, think, understand* and *want*. These verbs do not normally appear in the present continuous tense; e.g.

Teacher   Frederick* always understands me.
Student C   He understands you now (not *is understanding*).

*These names should be replaced by names of students in the class.

Step 2   *Telephone conversations between pairs of students.* Arrange the room so that pairs of students can hear but not see each other and small groups look for mistakes. A pair then

	pretends to telephone. You can give them a short time to prepare their conversation if you wish; e.g.
Student A	Hullo, is that B?
Student B	Yes, it is. Who's speaking?
Student A	It's A. I'm speaking from a telephone box in Portsmouth.
Student B	Oh! I didn't know ...

Game 19

Structures

Was)(*were*; e.g.
 Who *was*? ... What *was* ...? Who *were* ...? What *were* ...?

Structural Notes

Who and *what* can be followed by either *was* or *were*. They are followed by *was* if *he/she/it* or a singular noun/pronoun follows, e.g. *Who was I/he/she/it/that/that man?*; and by *were* if *we/you/they* or a plural noun/pronoun follows, e.g. *Who were we/you/they/those/those men?*

Materials
A set of cards with pictures or photographs.

Method

Step 1 Show a large picture or photograph for 30 seconds and then take it away. Now ask questions, leaving a blank for the verb; e.g.

Teacher (to A) Here is my first question.
Who — the man with the hat?

Student A Was.

Teacher (to B) What — the people doing?

Student B Were.

Step 2 Give a picture to a pair of students and ask them to take turns to ask *who* and *what* questions. After a short time the pictures can be exchanged with another pair.

Step 3 *Street interviews.* In each group of four, one student agrees to be the interviewer for a newspaper, or for a radio or television programme, and the other three agree to represent certain characters; they can be together or separate. The interviewer has to hold a short interview with these characters and to use as many of the structures in this game as possible.

Give each group time to work out and rehearse the interviews and let each team in turn give its interviews in front of the whole class. Agree beforehand on the means of deciding which is the best. This can be done by the teacher alone, by a separate group of judges, or by class reaction; e.g. by clapping or voting.

Game 20

Structures

I live here)(*I lived here*

Structural Notes

For the present simple tense, see Game 18.
   The past simple tense is used mostly for single or repeated action in the past when we are not interested in its present result (see Game 21 below); e.g. *I got up at seven yesterday*; *I got up at seven every day last week*.
   The present simple tense also usually replaces the present continuous tense for action going on at the time of speaking/writing when the verb is one of the so-called involuntary verbs; e.g. *know, understand, want*.

Materials

Lists of daily or weekly activities; e.g.
John
7.00 gets up
7.15 washes
7.30 has breakfast
8.00 leaves the house
Mrs Brown
Monday mornings: washes the clothes
Monday afternoons: dries the clothes
Monday evenings: goes to an English class
Tuesday mornings: irons the clothes

Method

Step 1 (a)   The teacher gets individual students to tell him what they or other people, e.g. the ones in the lists described in materials above, do regularly and what they did on, for instance, last Monday; e.g.

Teacher	What does John do at eight o'clock every day?
Student A	He leaves the house.
Teacher	What did he do at eight o'clock this morning?
Student B	He left the house.
Step 1 (b)	You can get students to ask the questions after you have asked a few yourself, and you can use *I* and *you* instead of other persons; e.g.
Teacher	What do you do at one o'clock every day, Helen?
Helen	I have lunch.
Teacher	What do I do at seven o'clock every evening?
Student B	You give a lesson.
Step 2	Get one student to make a statement about a habitual action, and another student to repeat the statement but to add a contradictory statement about a past occasion; e.g.
Student A	I usually go to the cinema in Brighton.
Student B	I usually go to the cinema in Brighton too, but last Saturday I went to the cinema in London.

Game 21

Structures

I opened the door)(*I have opened the door*

Structural Notes

For the past simple tense see Game 20, paragraph 2.
 The present perfect tense is used mostly for single or repeated action in the past when we are mainly interested in its present results; e.g. *Has Mary got up yet? How many times have you played tennis?*

Materials

1. Pictures showing actions which have been completed; e.g. a picture of a door which has been opened.
2. Sentences about these pictures with the verbs omitted; e.g. *John ... the door*.
3. Cards containing the missing verbs, in both the tenses given in Structures above; e.g. |HAS OPENED| |OPENED|. Alternatively, HAVE and HAS can be on separate cards so that they can be used with a variety of pictures.
4. Large sheets of paper, and crayons in bright colours.

Method

Step 1   The teacher points to one of the pictures mentioned in Materials 1 and gives the students one of the sentences mentioned in Materials 2. The students have to choose the correct cards to pu in the blank space in the sentence in order to make two ctorrect sentences; e.g.

John ... the door
Cards: |CLOSED| |OPENED| |HAVE| |HAVE| |HAS| |HAS|
Correct sentences: *John closed the door. John has opened the door.*

    You can also get the students to rewrite their two sentences in a better way; e.g. *John closed the door, but now he has opened it again.* You can give marks for correct sentences and also for the best rewritten ones.

Step 2   Divide the class into teams of four or five students. Ask each team to draw not more than three pictures (they can draw only one if they like) telling a story. The only writing allowed on each picture is the names and/or occupations of the people in it, the place and the time.

The pictures are now exchanged so that Team 1 is given Team 2's pictures, etc. The teams are given ten minutes to prepare to tell the story they see in the pictures. A rule is that the story must be told as if it happened in the past. The results are likely to amuse both the team which drew the pictures and the rest of the class.

While one team is telling the story in the pictures it has been given, the other teams have to observe its use of tenses. If they notice a mistake, they must draw attention to it. A team correctly noticing a mistake can be given a point which is deducted from the team which made the mistake.

Game 22

Structures

Past simple tense)(past perfect tense

Structural Notes

For the past simple tense, see Game 20 above.

The past perfect tense is used for actions which occurred before a certain time or event in the past; e.g. *When the train reached London, we ate our sandwiches* means 'First the train reached London, and then we ate our sandwiches' but *When the train reached London, we had eaten our sandwiches* means 'At the time at which the train reached London, the eating of our sandwiches was already in the past'.

Compare also *I finished my lunch at one* (the finishing happened at one) with *I had finished my lunch at one* (the finishing happened before one).

Materials

Lists of events in sequence of time, and/or picture stories giving sequences of events.

Method

Step 1	The teacher takes one of the lists of events or picture stories and asks questions whose answers require one of the tenses given under Structures above; e.g.
Teacher	Look at this list: *Yesterday afternoon*

> Mrs Smith had a bath
> Mr Smith came home
> Mrs Smith made some tea
> Mr and Mrs Smith drank it
> The newspaper boy came
> Mr Smith had a bath
> Mr Smith telephoned Mr and Mrs Jones
> Mr and Mrs Smith had dinner
> Mr and Mrs Jones arrived
> They all had coffee together

Teacher	What happened first?
Student A	Mrs Smith had a bath.
Teacher	What happened after that?
Student B	Mr Smith came home.
Teacher	What had Mrs Smith already done?
Student C	She had had a bath.

You can then put times opposite the various events, e.g. *5.00 Mrs Smith had a bath. 5.30 Mr Smith came home*, and ask further questions:

Teacher	What had already happened at 6.30?
Student B	At 6.30 Mrs Smith had had her bath, Mr Smith had come home, Mrs Smith had made some tea, and she and her husband had drunk it.
Step 2	So far, the teacher has given the student a clue to the correct tense to use in an answer by using that tense in the question. Now we go on to situations where such clues are not given.

The teacher, instead of asking questions, gives the students sentences with blanks instead of the verbs; e.g.

The newspaper boy ... when Mr and Mrs Smith ... their tea.

Student C	The newspaper boy came when Mr and Mrs Smith had drunk their tea.

Mr and Mrs Smith ... their dinner when Mr and Mrs Jones ...

Student D	Mr and Mrs Smith had had their dinner when Mr and Mrs Jones came.
Step 3	Students can now be made to ask questions like those in Step 1, or to make up sentences with blanks like those in Step 2. Other students can then give the answers.

Game 23

Structures

Present perfect tense)(present perfect continuous tense

Structural Notes

For the present perfect tense, see Game 21 above.
    The present perfect continuous tense usually indicates that the action began a certain time before the present moment and is not yet finished at the present moment. Contrast, for example, *I have cooked the lunch* with *I have been cooking the lunch for an hour* or *I have been cooking the lunch since 11.30*. In the first, the cooking finished some time before the moment of speaking; but in the other two sentences it is still going on at the moment of speaking.

Materials

As for Game 22 but with times given.

Method

Step 1
Teacher As in Game 22; e.g.
Look at this list: 10.00 John begins climbing a mountain
11.00 He reaches the top and begins looking at the view
11.15 He stops looking, sits down and begins his picnic meal
11.30 He finishes his food and lies down
11.31 He falls asleep
12.00 He wakes up and begins to go down the mountain again
12.45 He reaches the bottom

Teacher It is 11.10 now. What has John done?
Student A He has climbed to the top of the mountain and he has begun to look at the view.
Teacher How long has he been looking at it?
Student B He has been looking at it for 10 minutes.

Step 2	As in Game 22; or the teacher can just give a time and ask the student to say what has already happened and what is still going on at that time; e.g.
Teacher	It's 11.45 now.
Student C	John has climbed to the top of a mountain, looked at the view, eaten his meal, lain down and fallen asleep. He has been sleeping for 14 minutes.
Step 3	As in Game 22.

Game 24

Structures

Statements)(questions without question words)(questions with question words
(He) is here. Is he here? Where is he? I can see him. Can I see him? Who can see him? What can I see? You like it. Do you like it? Who likes it? What do you like? You liked it. Do you like it? Who liked it? What did you like?

Structural Notes

Question-words at this stage are *what/who/whom/whose/which/when/where/why/how*.

When a question has *what/who/whose/which* or a noun qualified by *what/whose/which* as its subject, the order of words is as in a statement; e.g. *I fell. Who fell? What fell? Which horse fell?*

In other questions which have a question-word and in questions which have no question-word, a verb precedes the subject; e.g. *Whom/What did you see? Where have you been?* If there is a special finite verb in a statement, it is put before the subject when the statement is turned into such a question; e.g. *You can help* becomes *Can you help? John is here* becomes *Is John here?* or *Where is John?* If there is no special finite, we use *do/does/did*; e.g. *The boys like it* becomes *Do the boys like it?* or *What do the boys like?*; *John likes it* becomes *Does John like it?*; and *John liked it* becomes *Did John like it?*

Materials

Pictures or very short stories, with answers to questions about them (see Step 1 below).

Method

Step 1

In this game, the teacher shows the students a picture or lets them read a very short story, and then gives them answers to questions about it. One student at a time has to provide the question which fits an answer; e.g.

Answer	He was in the sea.
Student A	Where was John?
Answer	He was swimming.
Student B	What was he doing?
Answer	Because he was hot.
Student C	Why was he in the sea?
Answer	Mary was.
Student D	Who was in the sea too?

Step 2

Twenty questions. Divide the class into teams of four. Each appoints a question-master who acts as chairman when his team is being questioned. Each team has to think of three people who are in the room or in the school or town, or likely to be well-known to most people.

Then Team 1 puts questions to Team 2 to try to discover the first person whom they are thinking of. Only questions to which a *Yes* or *No* is possible are allowed; e.g. *not* 'Has he black or brown hair?' but 'Is his hair black?'. The team which wins is the one which names the person correctly in less than 20 questions, or the one whose person is not guessed within 20. The teams move on so that Team 2 questions Team 3 and so on, and the winners play against each other in later games.

Game 25

Structures

Affirmative and negative tag questions

Structural Notes

After an affirmative statement, a tag question consists of a special finite + *-n't* + pronoun; e.g. *It's hot today, isn't it?*

After a negative statement, the *-n't* in the tag question is omitted, e.g. *John hasn't arrived yet, has he?*

If there is a special finite in the statement, this is repeated in the tag question; e.g. the two examples above and also *You have been there, haven't you? John can come, can't he?*

If there is no special finite in the statement we use *do/does/did* (see Game 24, last paragraph of Structural Notes); e.g. *You get up at seven, don't you? John gets up at seven, doesn't he? You got up at seven, didn't you?*

When the tag question is asked because one really wants an answer, the intonation pattern is a rising one; e.g. *You saw him, didn't you?*; but when the tag question is used only for politeness, a falling intonation pattern is used; e.g. *It's cold today, isn't it?*

Materials

A collection of pictures about which a variety of tag questions can be used. In addition to ones given in Structures above, there should be questions with *can, could, may, might, should, ought, shall, will, would, was, were, have, has, had, must, need, dare, used, do, does, did,* and *am, are, is.*

Method

Step 1   Make statements, some affirmative and some negative, about a picture and get students to echo them adding suitable tags; e.g.

Teacher	This man may be a clerk.
Student A	Yes, he may be one, mayn't he?
Teacher	But this one couldn't be a clerk.
Student B	No, he couldn't, could he?

Remember that a falling intonation should be used for such tag questions, which do not really ask for information.

Step 2	Get students to make the affirmative and negative statements and others to echo them. If too many affirmative statements are made and not enough negative ones, make it a rule that the two should alternate in the series of questions asked.
Step 3	Get students to make statements (affirmative and negative) followed by tag questions, and others to answer; e.g.
Student A	It's cold today, isn't it?
Student B	Yes, it is; *or* No, I don't think it is.

Remember that if the asker of the tag question *really* wants to know the answer (i.e. if he is really seeking information) he should use a rising intonation on the tag question (e.g. *This is the way to the station, isn't it?*), but if he is asking the question just to be polite, without really wanting an answer, he should use a falling intonation (see Step 1 above).

Game 26

Structure

Positions of adverbs of frequency

Structural Notes

Adverbs of frequency, e.g. *always, often, never*, are usually placed immediately before the verb if the verb consists of one part only, e.g. *I often go there*; but if the verb is part of the verb *to be*, the adverb of frequency follows it, e.g. *I am usually there*.

If the verb consists of two or more parts, the adverb of frequency usually comes immediately after the first of these; e.g. *I have never seen him. You can always see him there. I have sometimes been waiting for a whole hour when he arrives*

Materials

Collections of sentences; sets of cards, each containing one of the adverbs *always, ever, frequently, generally, never, often, rarely, seldom, sometimes* and *usually*. You need a set for each team.

Method

Step 1 — Divide the class into teams of about eight students each. Distribute the cards to the teams. Arrange your room as in the illustration:

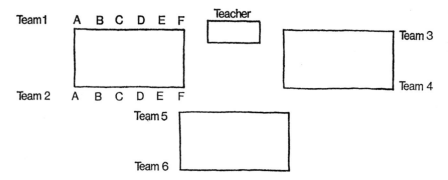

Members of each team draw a card in turn and have to use the word on it in one of the sentences supplied (see Materials above). Any member of the opposing team may challenge if he thinks the word has been used wrongly. The teacher can be the judge.

Some of the sentences should require the adverb to be put immediately before the verb, e.g. *I saw tigers in India*; others should require the adverb to be placed immediately after the verb, e.g. *I am ill*; and others should require it to be placed immediately after the first auxiliary verb, e.g. *I have seen tigers*; *At one o'clock we have been working for four hours*.

Once a particular sentence has been used, it cannot be used again by the same team.

Step 2   You can play the same game, but with the students making up their own sentences.

Game 27

Structures

So)(*not*)(*it*)(zero as clause-substitutes; e.g.
Is it raining? | I'm afraid | *so*
　　　　　　　　　　　　　　　| *not*
　　　　　　　　| I haven't noticed *it*
　　　　　　　　| I'll ask

Structural Notes

Certain verbs which can be followed by noun clauses replace these by *so/not* when a noun-clause substitute is required; e.g. '*Is George here?*' '*I hope so/not.*'*

Other verbs take *it* instead of *so/not* in such cases; e.g. '*Can you prove that you weren't here yesterday?*' '*Yes, I can prove it*'.*

Other verbs take nothing (zero); e.g. *'Can he do it?' 'I wonder.'**

Some verbs can take two or more of these substitutes according to the meaning; e.g. *tell* in *'I knew that John was going the wrong way'. 'Then why didn't you tell him?'** or *'Then why didn't you tell him so?'** *'Did John tell you that he was the best student at his university? He tells it** *to everyone.'*

*The clauses substituted are respectively: *that he is here/that he is not here; that I wasn't here yesterday; whether he can do it; that he was going the wrong way; that he was going the wrong way; that he is the best student at his university*).

Materials

Lists of statements and questions (see Method below); cards containing verbs which can be followed by one or more of the clause-substitutes given in Structures above.

Method

Divide the class into teams. Give each team a set of the cards mentioned in Materials above. The members of a team have to turn up the cards one by one and use the verbs on them to add comments to the statements or questions supplied; e.g.

Student A (drawing a card with *BELIEVE* on it, and choosing the sentence *Has John passed his examination?*): Has John passed his examination? I believe so; *or* I believe not.

Student B (drawing a card marked *WONDER* and choosing the sentence *Has it stopped raining?*): Has it stopped raining? I wonder.

Student C (drawing a card marked *DOUBT* and choosing the sentence *Mary is a very polite girl*): Mary is a very polite girl. I doubt it.

Instead of the same student making the statement and adding the comment, the members of a team can work in pairs, one drawing a card, both looking at it, one then choosing a sentence, and the other making the comment on it.

Game 28

Structures

Where's your pen? | Here | it is!
                     | *There* |
Where are your pens? | *Here* | they are!
                          | *There* |

Here's | your pen!
There's |

Here | *are* your pens!
There |

Structural Notes

When one sees or finds something and wants to exclaim about it, one can use the structure *here/there is/are*+noun, or *here/there*+pronoun+*is/are*; e.g. *Here's your pen! There are the boys! Here they are! There she is!*

Materials

Sets of 20 cards, each with the name of an object or the names of more than one object on them; pictures of the same objects or the objects themselves.

Method

Step 1	One student turns up a card and asks where the thing on the card is or where the things on the card are. Another student answers, using one of the structures given at the top of this page and at the same time pointing to the picture(s) of the object(s), or to the object(s) themselves if they are there; e.g.
Student A	(turning up the card marked *RUBBER*): Where's the rubber?
Student B	(pointing to it or its picture): There it is! [or, if it is close to him] Here it is!

By putting some of the objects or pictures near the students and others at some distance but still clearly visible, you can make them choose between *here* and *there* quite naturally.

Student C (turning up the card marked *THE TEACHER'S KEYS*): Where are the teacher's keys?

Student D Here they are! *or* There they are!

Student E (turning up the card marked *PENCIL AND PIECES OF PAPER*: Where's the pencil and the pieces of paper?

Student F Here's/There's the pencil, and here/there are the pieces of paper!

If the student who has to answer a question hesitates for too long, or answers incorrectly, he has to answer the next question too. But if he answers quickly and correctly he draws the next card and asks the next question.

Step 2 This is played in rather the same way as the game in Step 1, but there are no objects, only pictures of them, and these pictures are spread out face downwards on a table or other large flat surface.

When the student asking a question says '*Where's ... ?*', the student who has to answer says '*Here it is!*' or '*Here they are!*' and turns up one of the pictures. If he is right he takes the picture and keeps it; but if he is wrong he shows the picture to the other students and then puts it back carefully in the same place, face downwards again. One more student is now allowed to try to find the right picture. He too has to show the one he turns up to the other students and then put it back in the place he took it from.

After each question, the cards are shuffled and one is drawn by another student, who asks the question on it. A new student turns up one of the pictures in the hope of finding the right one. At first no one knows where the picture of a particular object is, but after the game has been played for a few minutes some of the students will remember where some of them are and be able to pick up the correct ones.

Game 29

Structures

What in exclamations)(*how* in exclamations

Structural Notes

Instead of exclaiming, for example, *That's a pretty hat!* one can say *What a pretty hat that is!* or just *What a pretty hat!* or *How pretty that hat is!* For other examples of these structures see Materials 1 below.

Materials

1. Examples of each of the structures; e.g.

What a big lake [that is]!	*How big that lake is!*
What big lakes [those are]!	*How big those lakes are!*
What dirty water [that is]!	*How dirty that water is!*
	How I hate rain!
	How nice!

2. Objects and pictures of objects which can be shown to the students to get them to make comments similar to those in Materials 1 above.

Method

Step 1   The teacher shows the students objects or pictures of objects or makes remarks, and points to one of the structures given in Materials 1 above. The students have to make comments on the objects, pictures or remarks, using the structure pointed to; e.g.

(The teacher points to the last structure in column 1 and shows a piece of very brightly coloured cloth)
Student A   What bright (*or* beautiful) cloth that is!
(The teacher points to a picture of a man doing the high jump and to the fourth structure in column 2)
Student B   How high that man is jumping!
Teacher   (pointing to the fourth structure in column 2): I'm going to give you all some ice-cream after the lesson.
Student C   How I love ice-cream!

51

Step 2	Divide the class up into two teams. These take turns to make one of the types of exclamation in the first three lines of the examples in Materials. The other team then has to turn the exclamation into the other type; e.g.
Team A	How big your nose is!
Team B	What a big nose you have!
Team B	What clean curtains those are!
Team A	How clean those curtains are!

Game 30

Structures

As much/many)(*more than*)(*the most*

Structural Notes

For the difference between *much* and *many* see Game 11 above.

As much/many as is used for comparisons of equality; e.g. *I have as much [money] as you have. John wants as many [bananas] as Mary has.*

More than and *the most* are used for comparisons of inequality; e.g. *I have more [money/bananas] than you have. John has the most [money/bananas].*

Materials

1. For Step 1 below: groups of objects (or pictures of these) varying in number/quantity; e.g. four plates of apples, one with two apples on it, two with three apples on each, and one with four apples; four bottles, one full of milk, two half full, and one almost empty.
2. For Step 2 below: instruction card.

Method

Step 1   Point to two of the groups in Materials 1 above, and get students to compare the numbers/quantities of things in them; e.g.

The teacher points to a boy (or a picture of a boy) holding two flags, and another also holding two.

Student A   John has got as many flags as Peter has.

The teacher points to two baskets, one full of meat and the other with less meat in it.

Student B   There is more meat in the basket on the left than in the one on the right.

The teacher points to three trees with varying numbers of leaves on them.

Student C   The tree in the middle has got more leaves than the one on the right. The tree on the left has got the most.

Step 2   The game can be continued in teams, with two at each table. Have a set of instructions for each leader, arrange the room, play and score as in Game 1, Step 2.

Game 31

Structures

Reported commands and requests

Structural Notes

Here is a common way of changing a command into the report of the command: Direct: *John said to Peter, 'Open the door.'* Report: *John told Peter to open the door.*

For changing a request into a reported request: Direct: *John said to Peter, 'Please open the door.'* Report: *John asked Peter to open the door.*

In a reported command/request, the person to whom the order is given or the request made must be mentioned; e.g. we cannot say *John told to open the door* although we can say *John said, 'Open the door'*. We also cannot use *say* instead of *tell* in the report; e.g. we cannot say *John said to open the door* or *John said Peter to open the door*. We also do not put a comma after *tell*+object; e.g. we do not put *John told Peter, to open the door.*

Materials

Lists of commands and requests.

Method

Step 1   The teacher gives various commands and makes various requests, and students have to pretend that they are deaf so that other students have to tell them what he said; e.g.

Teacher   Open the door, please, George.
Student A   What did the teacher say, George?
George   He asked me to open the door.
Teacher   Come here, Mary.
Mary   What did the teacher say, Helen?
Helen   He told you to go to his table.

Step 2 The class can now be divided into groups of three students who can then practise among themselves, taking turns to make the request or give the command, to be the deaf person, and to give the answer.

This game can develop into quite an amusing one if each group is allowed time to prepare a dialogue which is constantly interrupted by the 'deaf' person wanting to know what has been said. Each group can act its dialogue in front of the class and marks can be given for the most humorous, the most serious, the greatest misunderstanding, or the most convincing dialogue; e.g.

Student A Please make some tea.
Student B (the 'deaf' man): Did A ask you to shake his knee, C?
Student C No, he didn't. He asked me to make some tea.

Step 3 Divide the class into two teams. Each team must then form a line. The first student in each line whispers a command or request into the ear of the next one, who then has to whisper what he has heard into the ear of the next, and so on until the end of the line is reached. The last student has to say aloud what he thought his neighbour whispered to him, and the first student in the line then says aloud his original message.

Game 32

Structures

Reported statements

Structural Notes

Reported statements can be introduced by *said, said that,* or *told someone [that]*; e.g. *John said [that] it was raining* or *John told Peter [that] it was raining,* but not *John said Peter that it was raining* nor *John told that it was raining* nor *John told to Peter that it was raining.*

There should be no comma between the reporting verb and the report; e.g. one should not write *John said, [that] it was raining* nor *John told Peter, [that] it was raining.*

If the reporting verb is in a past tense, e.g. *said, was saying, used to say, had said,* the tenses in the direct speech move one step into the past; e.g. *do/does* becomes *did, am/are/is doing* becomes *was/were doing, did* becomes *had done, may do* becomes *might do.* If a verb is already in as 'past' a tense as is possible, it does not change any further; e.g. *had done* remains *had done,* and *would do* remains *would do.* If the reporting verb is in a present or future tense, e.g. *am/are/is saying, say/says, have/has said, shall/will say,* the tense remains the same in the report as it was in the direct statement.

Pronouns change when going from direct to reported speech according to the situation; e.g. *John said to Helen, 'I like Mary's new dress,'* if reported by Mary would be *John told Helen that he liked my new dress.* If reported by Helen to Mary it would be *John told me that he liked your new dress.*

There are also changes in certain other words when one goes from direct to reported speech and the introducing verb is in a past tense; e.g. *John said 'I was absent this morning'* becomes *John said that he had been absent that morning.* Mary said 'There is nobody here' becomes *Mary said that there was nobody there.*

Materials

Lists of statements.

Method

The same three steps can be used as in Game 31, except that statements take the place of commands and requests; e.g.

Step 1
Teacher	It's raining.
'Deaf' Student	What did he say, A?
Student A	He said that it was raining.
Teacher	You can't sit there, B.
'Deaf' Student	What did he tell you, B?
Student B	He told me that I couldn't sit here.

Step 2
Student C	It's really cool.
Student D	Did C say that you were a silly fool, E?
Student E	No, he didn't. He said that it was really cool.

Game 33

Structures

Reported questions

Structural Notes

There are two main types of direct questions: ones with a question-word and ones without one (see Game 24 above).

If a direct question has a question-word, this is kept in the report; e.g. *Peter said to John, 'What are you doing?'* becomes *Peter asked John what he was doing.* But if the direct question has no question-word we use *whether* or *if* in the report; e.g. *Peter said to John, 'Are you making a kite?'* becomes *Peter asked John whether/if he was making a kite.*

The order of words in a reported question is that of a statement, not that of a direct question; e.g. *John said, 'Is it raining?'* becomes *John asked whether/if it was raining,* not *John asked whether/if was it raining.*

The person who is asked the question can be mentioned in the report or not; e.g. one can say *Helen asked what I wanted* or *Helen asked me what I wanted.*

There is no question-mark in a reported question unless the reporting sentence is itself a question; e.g. *Mary said, 'Where are you going?'* becomes *Mary asked where (I) was going,* not *Mary asked where (I) was going?* But *Did Mary say, 'Where are you going?'* becomes *Did Mary ask (me) where I was going?*

There should be no comma between the reporting verb and the reported question; e.g. *Peter asked John how he was* not *Peter asked John, how he was.*

Materials

Write on the blackboard a number of questions to illustrate direct and indirect questions as in Structures above.

Method

Step 1   Get two, three or four students at a time to practise the dialogue with one of the questions on the board. In each case Student B pretends to be old and deaf; e.g.

(Two students)
Student A   Where is Mr Jones?
Student B   Eh? What did you say?
Student A   I asked you where Mr Jones was.
(Three students)
Student A (to B and C): Who can help me?
Student B (to C)   What did he say?
Student C   He asked me/you who could help him.
(Four students)
Student A (to D)   Why are you laughing?
Student B (to C)   What did A/he say?
Student C   He asked D why he was laughing.

Step 2   Arrange the room in rows with between five and eight people in each row.

The game is to see what happens to a question as it passes from one person to another. The rules are that each person must change the form of the question and that no one is allowed to repeat a statement or question. At the end of the row some of the messages will be very strange. The situation is intended to produce humour, but the teacher must be careful to see that the structures are

being practised correctly. If mistakes in the structure are being made, repeat Step 1; e.g.

Teacher (whispers to A, Row 1): Which is the road to London? (He then whispers another question to the As in other rows)
Student A (whispers to B): The teacher asked me which the road to London was.
Student B (whispers to C): The teacher asked A, 'Which is the road to London?'
Student C (to D)   The teacher asked A which the road to London was.
Student D (to E)   The teacher asked A, 'Which is the road to London?'

Repeat by moving everyone along one place (E moves to A's place). The teacher can take a seat so long as someone whispers a question to each row.

Game 34

Structures

Mixed reported speech

Structural Notes

When statements, requests, commands and questions follow each other in reported speech, the same general rules apply as for the individual kinds of reported speech (see Games 31 to 33 above) but one must also be careful to introduce each type suitably; e.g. *John said, 'Come in. What do you want? I'll get you a chair'* becomes *John told Peter to come in, asked [him] what he wanted and said [that] he would get him a chair.*

Materials

Short conversations containing mixtures of commands, requests, statements and questions (see Games 31–33).

Method

As in Game 31, except that all kinds of reported speech introduced in games 31–33 can be used; e.g.

Step 1

Teacher	Come in, George. What do you want? I haven't got much time.
'Deaf' Student	What did the teacher tell George?
Student A	He told him to come in, asked him what he wanted and told him that he hadn't got much time.

Game 35

Structures

Must do)(*have to do*)(*have got to do*)(*will have to do*)(*had to do*)(*had got to do*

Structural Notes

Must indicates obligation imposed by the speaker/writer; e.g. *I must go now : I don't want to be late.*

Have/has to and *have/has got to* indicates obligation imposed by someone/ something other than the speaker/writer; e.g. *I have to go now* or *I've got to go now : my train leaves in 20 minutes' time.*

Shall/will have to is the future of *must, have/has to* and *have/has got to*; e.g. *I shall have to leave at 10 tomorrow; had to* and *had got to* are their past simple forms; e.g. *I had to leave at 10 yesterday. I was told that I'd got to leave at 10.*

Materials
Lists of sentences; two octagonal 'tops' for each team.
You can make these tops by folding a piece of paper in half:

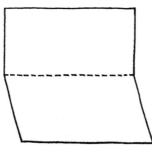

Then folding in half again:

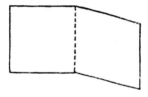

and then folding diagonally:

Now measure 7 cm. along the edges of the triangle which are nearest to the point which will be the centre of the 'top', draw a line to join the two 7 cm. marks, and then cut along this line. Open out your piece of paper, which will now look like this: (the dotted lines represent folds).

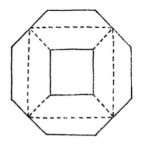

Then stick this shape on to strong cardboard and cut round it with a sharp knife or scissors.

Mark the following on half of your 'tops': And mark the following on the other half:

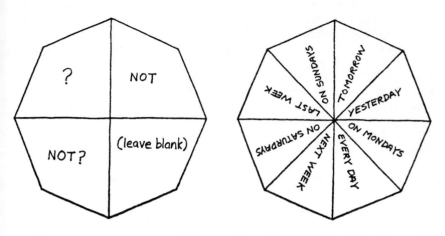

If you now push a short pencil through the exact centre of each 'top', you will be able to spin it:

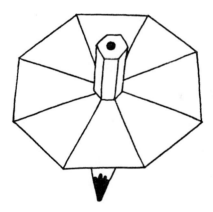

Method

Step 1 Divide the class up into teams. Give each team two 'tops' (one of each kind). Teams now have to take turns to spin their two 'tops'. If the one with the question-marks and NOT's on it stops with the side marked NOT nearest the table, the team has to make a negative sentence. If the question-mark is lowest, they have to make a question. If NOT? is lowest, they have to make a negative interrogative sentence; and if the blank side is lowest, an affirmative statement.

When the other 'top' is spun, the word which is lowest when the 'top' stops has to be included in the sentence.

The sentences are built up from the teacher's lists (see Materials above); e.g. the next sentence on the teacher's list is: *get up at 6 a.m.* and one team's 'tops' stop at *NOT* and *YESTERDAY*.

Student A I didn't have to get up at 6.00 a.m. yesterday; *or* I hadn't got to get up at 6.00 a.m. yesterday.

If the 'tops' stop at the question-mark and *TOMORROW*:

Student B Will you have to get up at 6.00 a.m. tomorrow?
Student C Yes, I will; *or* No, I won't.

If the 'tops' stop at *NOT?* and *ON MONDAYS*:

Student D Don't you have to get up at 6.00 a.m. on Mondays?
Student E Yes, I do; *or* No, I don't.

Step 2 The teams can now be asked to make up their own sentences like those in Materials above, and to continue playing the game with the 'tops' against each other.

Game 36

Structures

Can do)(*will be able to do*)(*was able to do*)(*has been able to do*

Structural Notes

Can indicates present or future ability; e.g. *I can see a ship now. I can help you tomorrow.*

Shall/will be able to indicates future ability; e.g. *I'll be able to help you tomorrow.*
Was/were able to indicates past ability; e.g. *I was able to help John yesterday.*
Have/has been able to is the present perfect of *can do* (see Game 21 above); e.g.
I have often been able to help Henry.

Materials
Pictures, parts of which can be covered (see Step 1 below); a record player or tape-recorder; things which have definite smells and tastes; stories (see Step 1).

Method

Step 1   The teacher allows the students to see, hear, feel, smell and taste various things; e.g. the teacher shows a picture in which there is a girl.

Teacher   Can you see this girl?
Student A   Yes, I can.
Teacher   (covering the picture of the girl): Can you see her now?
Student B   No, I can't.
Teacher   Were you able to see her a moment ago?
Student C   Yes, I was.
Teacher   I'm going to uncover her soon. Will you be able to see her?
Student D   Yes, I will.

The teacher uncovers the picture and counts: one, two, three, four, etc.

Teacher   How long have you been able to see her now?
Student E   I've been able to see her for (ten) seconds.

The teacher can do the same with hearing, smelling, tasting and feeling; e.g. he plays the tape-recorder, stops it and then says he is going to start it again; he puts a rose near a student's nose, takes it away and then says he is going to put it near his nose again; he gives a student something to eat, then gives him something with a stronger taste (*I was able to taste the sugar, but now I can't taste it. I can only taste the vinegar*); he gives a student something he can feel, then takes it away.

Other verbs can be used too, especially if stories are used; e.g. in a story, we are told that the ceiling in a room is seven feet high. We are also told that when Johnny was ten, he was three feet high, but when he was sixteen, he was six feet high. The teacher can ask such questions as *Was Johnny able to touch the ceiling when he was ten? He's sixteen now. Can he touch the ceiling?*

Step 2   So far the teacher has been using the tenses himself in his questions so that the students know what tense to use in each answer. Now we go on to the next step where the teacher does not give any clues. He does the same kinds of things as in Step 1, but now the students have to make statements. The teacher can put a list of adverbs on the blackboard and point to one of them whenever he wants a student to make a statement. The student then has to include that adverb in his statement; e.g.

The teacher puts some pepper near a student's nose.
Student F   I can smell that pepper.
The teacher takes it away.
Student F   I can't smell it now.
The teacher (if the student doesn't give the next answer himself) points to the adverb *a few moments ago*.
Student F   I was able to smell the pepper a few moments ago.

Step 3   Divide the class into groups of about five. Each group has to prepare and then act a scene with the following characters in it:

An important person; e.g. a politician, or a manager
His wife
His secretary
Two impatient visitors

They have to use the structures as often as possible. You can have a scoring system to give a point for each correct use of one of the structures. Points can also be given for good, lively acting.

Game 37

Structures

Ought to do)(*should do*)(*ought to have done*)(*should have done*

Structural Notes

Ought to and *should* indicate moral obligation or desirability; e.g. *We ought to/should help the poor. You ought to/should be more careful when you cross the road*

Ought to have and *should have*+past participle indicate moral obligation or desirability in the past, usually with the suggestion that the action was not in fact carried out; e.g. *You ought to/should have given that poor man some money. You ought to/should have been more careful when you crossed the road.*

Materials
Sentences which get the students to use the above structures (see Method below).

Method

Step 1   The teacher should give a student a sentence and the student should then make a comment about it which contains one of the structures given above; e.g.

Teacher   I know a very poor man.
Student A   You ought to give him some money; *or* You should give him some money.
Student B   You should give him some money; *or* (if Student A has already said that) You ought to give him some money.
Teacher   I knew a very poor man five years ago.
Student C   You ought to (*or* should) have given him some money.
Student D   You should (*or* ought to, whichever C has not used) have given him some money.

When the teacher talks about the present the first student should answer with the *ought to do* or *should do* tense and the second one should answer with whichever of these tenses the first student did not use. But if the teacher talks about the past the two students should answer with the *ought to have done* and *should have done* tenses.

Step 2   The students are asked to make up their own statements in place of the teacher. One student makes a statement, another answers using one of the structures and a third then uses the other structure, as in Step 1 above.

Game 38

Structures

May do)(*may be doing*)(*may have done*)(*may have been doing*

Structural Notes

May indicates future possibility, habitual possibility, or, in the case of 'involuntary' verbs*, present possibility; e.g. *It may rain tomorrow. John may have a bath every day. Mary may already know the answer now.*

May be+*-ing* form indicates present possibility; e.g. *It may be raining in London now.*

May have+past participle indicates past possibility; e.g. *It may have rained in London yesterday.*

May have been+*-ing* form indicates the possibility that something was happening at a given moment in the past; e.g. *It may have been raining at 11.00 a.m. yesterday. John may have been working in the garden when you telephoned him yesterday.*

May can also be used to indicate permission; e.g. *You may go now*; but it is not used with this meaning in this game.

*Cf. Game 20 above, present simple tense.

Materials

Sentences which the teacher can give the students, to get them to use the above structures (see Step 1 below); one pack of cards for each group.

Method

Step 1   The teacher makes statements or asks questions and the students reply, using one of the structures given above; e.g.

Teacher   Why is Mr Smith taking an umbrella? It isn't raining now.
Student A   No, but it may rain soon.

Teacher	Why is Mrs Smith running upstairs to see her baby?
Student B	It may be crying.
Teacher	Why is the street wet this morning?
Student C	It may have rained last night.
Teacher	Why did Sally look out of the window and then decide not to go out yesterday?
Student D	It may have been raining.

Step 2 Students are asked to take the place of the teacher and make the statements or ask the questions. Other students then have to make the comments, using the structures. If one of the students who have to make comments thinks that is impossible to make one using one of the structures, he can challenge the student who made the statement or asked the question. The person challenged then has to make a suitable comment himself. If he can do so, he gets two points. If he can't, his challenger gets two. The teacher is the judge of whether the challenged student has given an acceptable answer; e.g.

Student E	Do you like coffee?
Student F	I challenge you to answer that one.
Student E	I may like it tomorrow.
Teacher	No, E, I don't think that is a reasonable answer. I'll give two points. Try to ask questions which can easily be answered with one of our structures.

Step 3 Divide the class into groups of five or six students. Give each group a pack of ordinary playing-cards. Each group's pack should be dealt out among the members of the group.

Each player in turn turns up one of his cards and puts it on the table face up. The card shows which of the four structures given in Structures above he must make a sentence with. If a player turns up an ace, a five or a nine, he must use the first structure (*may do*); a two, six or ten means the second structure (*may be doing*); a three, seven or jack means the third structure (*may have done*); and a four, eight, queen or king means the fourth structure (*may have been doing*).

The other members of the group may accept or reject the sentence a student has made. Let us imagine that Student G has to make a sentence with *may have done*. He makes a sentence but H claims that it is incorrect (i.e. either that it does not contain this structure, or that there is a mistake in the sentence). He then has to correct the sentence and the teacher is then called to judge between G and H. If he agrees with G, G gives one of his cards to H, who puts it at the bottom of his cards. If the teacher agrees with H, H gives one of his cards to G, who also puts it under his other cards. If both G and H are wrong, the card remains on the table.

The first player to get rid of all his cards, or the player who has least when the teacher ends the game, is the winner.

Game 39

Structures

If)(*when*

Structural Notes

In the sentence *When John comes in, give him this letter*, the speaker is sure that John will come in; but in *If John comes in, give him this letter*, he is not sure. The first sentence means 'John is going to come in. At the time that he does come in, give him this letter'. The other sentence means 'Perhaps John will come in and perhaps he won't. In the former event, give him this letter'.

Materials

Lists of sentences containing *if* and *when*, but written with these words omitted.

Method

Step 1   The teacher gives a student one of the sentences mentioned in Materials above, and the student has to read it out, putting in *if* or *when* (or if either is possible he should read the sentence twice, once with *if* and once with *when*). After that the same student (or, if the teacher prefers, another one) should explain what the sentence means. If the first student has read the sentence twice the student giving the meaning should deal with both readings, one after the other; e.g.

Teacher (pointing to: . . . it rained tomorrow, I would be very surprised): A.

Student A If it rained tomorrow, I would be very surprised.

Student A (or B) This means: I don't think it will rain tomorrow, but it is possible. If it does rain, I will be surprised.

Teacher (pointing to: I will go home . . . I finish my lessons): C.

Student C I will go home when I finish my lessons.

Student C (or D) This means: I will finish my lessons, and after that I will go home.

Teacher (pointing to: I will see you . . . I come to your house): E.

Student E I will see you if I come to your house. I will see you when I come to your house.
Student E (or F) I will see you if I come to your house means: Perhaps I will come to your house, and perhaps I will not. If I do, I will see you. I will see you when I come to your house means: I will come to your house, and I will see you at that time.

Step 2 Divide the class into small groups, three or four students in each. Give each group 15 minutes to write a short story containing examples of *if* and *when* but leaving blanks whenever these occur. After 15 minutes groups exchange stories and fill in the blanks in the one they have received. Where they think that both *if* and *when* are possible, they put in both.

Each group then reads the story it has dealt with aloud to the rest of the class. Any member of the group which wrote the story in the first place can challenge the way a blank has been filled in. If the challenge is correct, he gets two points. If it is wrong, he loses two. A point is given for each correct filling of a blank.

When a challenge is made, the challenger has to explain what the sentence which he thinks incorrect would mean, and the defending group has to explain what meaning it gives to the sentence itself. The teacher is the final judge.

Game 40

Structures

Conditional sentences of the following types:
I will help him if he wants)(*I would help him if he wanted*)(*I will be bathing at ten o'clock if it isn't raining*)(*I would be bathing now if I was at home*)(*I would have helped him if he had wanted*)(*I would have been bathing if I had been at home*

Structural Notes

One can have past conditions, present conditions, ordinary future conditions and improbable future conditions; one can also have past results, present results, future results of ordinary conditions, and future results of improbable conditions; e.g.

Past condition+past result: *If you had come yesterday, I would have given you some cakes.*
Present condition+present result: *If you were working now, you wouldn't be feeling bored.*
Ordinary future condition+future result: *If I see your brother tomorrow, I'll give him your books.*
Improbable future condition+future result: *If that rope broke, you would fall.*

It is possible to have a past condition with a present or future result, and a present condition with a future result; e.g. *If you had worked harder last term, you wouldn't be worrying about your examinations now. If you had worked harder last term, you would pass them easily next week. If I was living in a hot country, I would go for a swim in the sea tomorrow.*

Materials

Lists of sentences which get the students to use the above structures (see Step 1 below).

Method

Step 1	The teacher asks the students questions using one of the structures given above; e.g.
Teacher	The Director may want some help tomorrow. What will you do if he wants it?
Student A	If he wants it, I will help him.
Teacher	It might rain tomorrow. What would you do if it did?
Student B	If it rained, I would bring my umbrella to school.
Teacher	I am planning to sunbathe from two to four tomorrow afternoon if the sun is shining then. What will I be doing at three if it is?
Student C	You will be sunbathing if the sun is shining.
Teacher	I am always watching television at this time when I am at home. What would I be doing now if I was at home?
Student D	You would be watching television if you were at home.
Teacher	I was willing to teach you yesterday but there was no lesson. What would I have done if there had been one?
Student E	You would have taught us if there had been a lesson.
Teacher	I am always having lunch when my mother comes to visit me on Sundays, but last Sunday I was not hungry. What would I have been doing when she came if I had been hungry?

Student F	You would have been having lunch if you had been hungry.
Step 2	So far, the teacher has been giving the students clues by using the tenses himself in his questions. Now we go on to the next stage, where the teacher does not give such clues; e.g.
Teacher	Perhaps John will want some help tomorrow.
Student G	I will help him if he wants.
Teacher	Mary hates getting wet. She has been invited to a picnic tomorrow. It may rain, but I think it is very improbable.
Student H	Mary wouldn't go if it rained.
Teacher	I never bathe in the rain. I am planning to bathe from nine to eleven tomorrow morning, but it may rain. Tell me something about ten o'clock, C.
Student I	You will be bathing at ten o'clock if it isn't raining.
Teacher	I am usually reading at this time when I am at home.
Student J	You would be reading now if you were at home.
Teacher	I was willing to help the Director last Sunday, but he didn't ask me to.
Student K	You would have helped him if he had asked you.
Teacher	I am usually sleeping when the clock strikes midnight, but last night I was ill so I was awake.
Student L	You would have been sleeping if you hadn't been ill.
Step 3	*Heads and Tails.* Divide the class up into groups of three students. Each student in the group has to write six sentences, one using each of the structures. While this is going on, the teacher goes around checking. The sentences are then split, the main clause being written on one card or piece of paper, and the *if*-clause on another. This pack of 36 'cards' is now shuffled and handed over to another group which has to re-join the heads and tails correctly.

Note that (a) a head may sometimes also fit a different tail from the one the first group intended it to fit; and (b) the heads and tails can be put in either order (i.e. the *if*-clause can precede *or* follow the main clause).

When a group has finished rejoining the clauses, it hands the pack back to the group which prepared it, who then say which sentences are right and which are wrong. The teacher is the final judge in case of disagreement.

Index

The numbers refer to the games in which the structures appear

able
  able to do 36
adjectives 14
  comparison 13
adverbs 14
  comparison 13
  here and *there* in *Here/There (it) (is)*!
    and *Here/There (is) (the bus)*! 28
  of frequency 26
any
  in negative sentences and questions 10
articles
  definite 1, 3
  indefinite 1, 2
  no article 2, 3
as
  as much/many 30

be 5, 16, 19

can 36
clause-substitutes
  it 27
  not 27
  so 27
  zero 27
commands
  reported commands 31
comparatives 13, 30
comparisons
  of equality 30
  of superiority 30

conditionals 39, 40

exclamations
  with *how* 29
  with *what* 29

far
  in negative sentences and questions 15
feminine 8
a few 12
frequency
  adverbs of frequency 26

gender 8

have/has
  had got to do 35
  had to do 35
  have/has got to do 35
  have/has to do 35
  will have to do 35
he 8
here
  in *Here (is) (the bus)*! 28
  in *Here (it) (is)*! 28
how
  in questions 24
  in exclamations 29

if 39, 40
it
  as clause-substitute 27

little
  a little 12
long (adj.)
  a long time 15
  a long way 15
long (adv.)
  replacing *a long time* in negative sentences and questions 15
lot
  a lot (of) 11

many
  as many 30
  replacing *a lot (of)* in negative sentences and questions 11
masculine 8
may
  may be doing 38
  may do 38
  may have been doing 38
  may have done 38
more 13, 30
most 13, 30
much
  as much 30
  replacing *a lot (of)* in negative sentences and questions 11
must 35

negatives
  far in negative sentences 15
  long in negative sentences 15
  many in negative sentences 11
  much in negative sentences 11
  not as clause-substitute 27
none 10
not
  as clause-substitute 27
nouns
  countable 1, 2
  definite 1
  indefinite 1, 2
  possessive 7
  uncountable 2
  number 5, 16

object 6
ought to
  ought to do 37
  ought to have done 37

76

person 16, 17
  third person, present simple tense 17
plurals 4, 5, 16
  unchanged 4
  with *pieces of* 4
  with *-s* 4
positive 13
possessive 7
pronouns
  feminine 8
  masculine 8
  personal 6, 8
  possessive 7
  with *-self/-selves* 9
  without *-self/-selves* 9

questions
  far in questions 15
  long in questions 15
  many in questions 11
  much in questions 11
  reported questions 33
  tag questions 25
  without questions words 24
  with question words 5, 24

reported speech 31, 32, 33, 34
requests
  reported 31

-self/-selves 9
she 8
should
  for obligation or desirability 37
  should do 37
  should have done 37
singular 5, 16
so
  as clause substitute 27
some 10
statements 24
  reported 32
subject 6
superlative 13, 30

tag questions 25
tenses
  future 35, 36
  past 19, 20, 21, 22, 35, 36, 37, 38
  past of *be* 19
  past perfect 22

past simple   20, 21, 22
present   5, 16, 17, 18, 20, 35, 38
present continuous   18, 38
present of *be*   5, 16
present perfect   21, 23
present perfect continuous   23, 38
present simple   17, 18, 20
there (adv)
   There (is) (the bus)!   28
   There (it) (is)!   28

what
   in exclamations, 29

   in questions   5, 19, 24
when
   in questions   24
   introducing clauses of time   39
where
   in questions   24
which
   in questions   24
who
   in questions   5, 16, 19, 24
whose
   in questions,   24
why
   in questions   24

Bibliography

Further information about the grammatical points can be obtained from the following books:

A. S. Hornby – A Guide to Patterns and Usage in English (OUP, 1954)
W. S. Allen – Living English Structure (Longman, 1947)
L. A. Hill – Elementary, Intermediate and Advanced Refresher Courses (OUP, 1964–5)
L. A. Hill – Prepositions and Adverbial Particles (OUP, 1968)